ASK THE
CONSTITUTION

Can Anyone Own a Gun?

Jeff Mapua

D1716287

Enslow Publishing
101 W. 23rd Street
Suite 240
New York, NY 10011
USA
enslow.com

Published in 2020 by Enslow Publishing, LLC.
101 W. 23rd Street, Suite 240, New York, NY 10011

Library of Congress Cataloging-in-Publication Data

Names: Mapua, Jeff, author.
Title: Can anyone own a gun? / Jeff Mapua.
Description: New York : Enslow Publishing, 2020. | Series: Ask the Constitution | Includes bibliographical references and index.
Identifiers: LCCN 2018048404| ISBN 9781978507135 (library bound) | ISBN 9781978508378 (pbk.)
Subjects: LCSH: Firearms—Law and legislation—United States—Juvenile literature. | Gun control—United States—Juvenile literature.
Classification: LCC KF3941 .M329 2019 | DDC 344.7305/33—dc23
LC record available at https://lccn.loc.gov/2018048404

Printed in the United States of America

To Our Readers: We have done our best to make sure all website addresses in this book were active and appropriate when we went to press. However, the author and the publisher have no control over and assume no liability for the material available on those websites or on any websites they may link to. Any comments or suggestions can be sent by email to customerservice@enslow.com.

Contents

Introduction

The United States is a large country. There are many people who live in each of the country's fifty states. What many people may not know, however, is that there are enough guns for every man, woman, and child to own one for themselves. After that, there would be 67 million guns left over.

The Graduate Institute of International and Development Studies in Geneva conducted a Small Arms Survey. The project took data and surveys from 230 countries. The survey looked at civilians, or people not belonging to the armed services or police. It found that most of the firearms or guns in the world are in the United States. In 2017, there were 393 million guns in the United States. This makes up 46 percent of the 857 million civilian firearms in the whole world.[1]

The country with the second most number of civilian firearms is India. However, with 71.1 million guns, India has more than five times fewer guns than the United States. In terms of guns per 100 people, the United States again has more guns than any other country. The survey revealed 120.5 guns per 100 people in the United States. In comparison, Yemen had the second highest rate of guns per 100 civilians at 52.8. That is less than half of the United States.[2]

The United States has a long history of gun ownership. The right to own firearms is written into the very fabric of the government. People have fought over who can own a gun and what types of guns are allowable for civilians to own. Many people have passionate views on how guns should fit into American society and culture.

This passion helped fuel the increase in the number of guns owned in the United States. When President Barack Obama was elected, many feared that guns would be taken away from US citizens. The popular opinion among gun owners was that President Obama would introduce laws that would reduce the number and type of guns they could own. America's gun manufacturers responded to these fears by doubling their output between 2009 and 2013. The Small Arms Survey found that US civilians added more than 122 million firearms from 2006 to 2017.[3]

However, the crackdown on guns never happened. People stockpiled weapons in fear of new laws that never materialized. The result was the eye-popping gun ownership statistics found by the Small Arms Survey. Additionally, the survey found that guns were not spread evenly across US citizens. This means that those who owned guns owned most of the guns. In 2017, the average gun-owning household owned almost eight guns.[4]

These and similar findings by other studies are alarming to many people who are against firearms. And with the strong support of firearms by gun advocates, the United States is all but guaranteed a long and hard-fought battle over who can own guns in America.

1

The Constitution

All Americans in the United States must follow the laws created by the government. Some laws tell people what they cannot do, such as stealing or driving faster than the speed limit. Other laws protect citizens from the government. The oldest laws in America come from the Constitution.

What Is the Constitution?

The United States of America is governed by laws. The supreme law of the land is found in the Constitution. The Constitution was the second attempt at forming a government by the founders of the United States. The first attempt, the Articles of Confederation, proved to have too many problems, the biggest being that the central government did not have enough power to properly run the country.[1]

In 1787, representatives from the thirteen states, except for Rhode Island, came together to redesign the government. The meeting was called the Constitutional Convention. They established the three branches of government—the legislative, executive, and judicial branches—and what powers each had. The legislative branch makes the laws, the executive branch enforces laws, and the judicial branch includes the court system and interprets the laws. The Constitution also specified what powers the states held and what powers the federal, or national, government held.[2]

The Founding Fathers gathered to sign the Constitution of the United States. Traditionally, the Founding Fathers include Alexander Hamilton, John Adams, Benjamin Franklin, John Jay, Thomas Jefferson, James Madison, and George Washington.

One major concern for the Founding Fathers of the country was giving too much power to the government or to a single branch. The people of the young United States had escaped the rule of the king of England. They did not want to find themselves in the same position again. By establishing three equal branches of government, the representatives at the Constitutional Convention believed they achieved this goal.[3]

What Is the Bill of Rights?

During the Constitutional Convention, the founders were careful to decide on the process to make changes to the Constitution. This would ensure that new laws could be introduced when the need arose. When the states were asked to approve the new Constitution, many people asked for the creation of a bill of rights. This would name basic civil rights that all citizens would have.[4]

Reasons for the Revolutionary War

The Revolutionary War took place from 1775 through 1783. The war was between American colonists and the British Empire. After a hard-fought war, the North American colonies won independence and formed the United States of America.

The Revolution happened because colonists felt they were treated unfairly. One example was taxes that people in England did not have to pay. These included the Stamp Tax, a tax on newspapers and marriage licenses, and a tax on tea. Colonists were upset that no one represented them in the British government. Without representation, the colonists were powerless to make changes to help themselves. They argued that they should not be ruled by a king 3,000 miles (4,828 kilometers) away. Colonists believed in self-government, which was later reflected in the Constitution.[5]

James Madison introduced twelve amendments to the Constitution. Ten were passed and are called the Bill of Rights. They contain rights that many consider fundamental to America.[6]

The First Amendment protects the freedom of speech and the press. It also gives people the right to assemble and to petition the government when they feel they have been wronged in some way by the state or country. Other amendments include rights such as due process, or being fairly treated by the judicial system, and a speedy trial by a jury of one's peers. Other amendments protect citizens from the government in various ways. These include protection against being searched without a warrant, from having troops or soldiers stationed in people's homes, and from cruel and unusual punishments.[7]

The Second Amendment specifically addresses the rights citizens have to firearms. It is the amendment that answers the question of who can own a gun in the United States.

What Is the Second Amendment?

The Second Amendment says, "A well-regulated Militia being necessary to the security of a free State, the right of the people to keep and bear Arms shall not be infringed."[8] At first glance, the amendment states that militias are necessary to protect US citizens. It also states that the government is not allowed to prohibit people from keeping and owning firearms. However, there is great debate over the intention of the Founding Fathers.

People continue to argue today about what rights the writers of the Constitution meant for the Second Amendment to actually protect. Some believe in what is known as the "individual right theory." The individual right theory states that the phrase "the right of the people

JAMES MADISON

James Madison introduced twelve articles to the Constitution; the ten that were approved would come to be known as the Bill of Rights.

to keep and bear Arms" means that each person must be allowed to own guns. People who believe in this theory say that the government is restricted from prohibiting, or formally forbidding something by law, rule, or other authority, the possession of firearms.[9]

On the other side of the debate, people believe in the "collective rights theory." This theory stems from the phrase "a well-regulated Militia." People

What the Second Amendment meant when it was written, and what it means to gun owners today, is a source of constant debate.

believe that this portion of the amendment is evidence that the Founding Fathers only meant to protect a state's right to self-defense. The theory states that citizens in the United States do not actually have the right to own guns. Instead, the government at local, state, and federal levels can regulate who can own guns without violating the Constitution.[10]

There are many arguments for and against each theory. The debate is far from over and has only increased in intensity as gun violence has become a bigger issue. Without the Founding Fathers around to say exactly what they meant in the Second Amendment, the debate will continue.

The Gun Amendment

The Second Amendment is the only law set forth by the Founding Fathers that addresses gun ownership. Over the years many people, such as lawyers, judges, and scholars, have tried to uncover the original intent of the amendment. There are things the amendment protects and others it does not.

The Second Amendment Today

There is a long history of the Second Amendment in the court system. Over the years since it was introduced, the Second Amendment, and how it is seen by people, evolved. In the 1875 court case of *United States v. Cruikshank*, the United States Supreme Court said that the Second Amendment "has no other effect than to restrict the powers of the national government."[1] This meant that they believed that while the federal government was not allowed to regulate guns, the states were free to do so if they pleased. This viewpoint was supported in a later 1886 case, *Presser v. Illinois*. Here the Supreme Court said that the Second Amendment "is a limitation only upon the power of Congress and the National government, and not upon that of the States."

When the Second Amendment was written, assault rifles like these didn't exist. Have modern weapons changed the historical context of the Constitution?

The Second Amendment was further defined in the 1939 case *United States v. Miller*. A sawed-off shotgun was transported between states, and it was determined that Congress had the power to regulate this action. The court argued that the shotgun did not have a reasonable relationship to keeping a well-regulated militia. The court further added that it believed the Second Amendment was meant to ensure the effectiveness of the military.[2]

This was how it remained for almost seventy years until *District of Columbia v. Heller* in 2008. For thirty-two years, there was a handgun ban in Washington, DC. The ban was challenged by police officer Dick

Heller. The Supreme Court agreed with Heller and decided the handgun ban violated the Second Amendment, which allowed individuals to own handguns. It was clear that the Supreme Court believed in the individual right theory. However, the court said that the government was allowed to place regulations on criminals and the mentally ill from owning firearms.[3]

Assault Weapons

With the *Heller* decision, the Second Amendment was strengthened. It was further strengthened in 2010's *McDonald v. City of Chicago,* which stated that the Second Amendment applies to the states, too, and Illinois was not allowed to ban handgun ownership.

However, there are some things that are not covered by the amendment, such as gun ownership for criminals and the mentally ill. In *District of Columbia v. Heller,* Supreme Court justice Antonin Scalia said that although the Second Amendment allows individuals to own firearms, this right "is not unlimited."[4] This was specifically true for assault weapons. An assault weapon is any one of the many different styles of automatic or semiautomatic firearms. This is the definition recognized by the federal government and refers to military-style weapons that can fire multiple rounds in either semiautomatic or fully automatic settings. Many gun supporters disagree with this definition as something created by antigun activists. Gun supporters believe that guns don't actually assault people.[5]

The argument over this definition is vital to the AR-15 rifle. This rifle is considered by the government to be an assault rifle. But since the AR-15 is only capable of semiautomatic settings and is not fully automatic, gun advocates, or supporters, argue that this means AR-15s are not assault weapons.[6]

In 2017, a federal court found that the state of Maryland was allowed to ban assault weapons. It was the fourth time that a federal court ruled that bans on assault weapons are constitutional. Each time, the court argued that the ban did not affect people's right to defend themselves since there are other weapons available for people to own. The federal courts also argued that states and cities can ban AR-15-style weapons because of the dangers they pose to public spaces, people, and the police.[7]

Armed Militias

The Second Amendment makes special mention of a "well-regulated Militia" as being an important part of securing a free state or country. What is considered a militia has changed over the years to adapt to modern times. During the American Revolutionary War, a militia was a group of men who protected their town or colony. Whereas today a militia is often considered to be unaffiliated with the government, a militia in the late 1700s was a state-based institution. This means that states organized these groups themselves.[8]

The Supreme Court of the United States hears many arguments involving the Second Amendment; here, Otis McDonald speaks after winning *McDonald v. City of Chicago.*

The AR-15 rifle has been a source of contention in recent years, given its use in mass shootings across the United States.

Another part of the amendment that has changed definition over time is the phrase "well-regulated." Today, people understand well-regulated to mean that the state or government controlled the militia in some way. The eighteenth-century definition of "well-regulated" was to be well-organized, armed, and disciplined. It meant that militias would be prepared to perform their duty.[9]

What is not as clear, however, is what the Founding Fathers intended regarding militias and firearms. Were guns meant only for people who were in an official militia? Did they mean to allow people to own guns

American Viewpoints

Gun rights and ownership is a fiercely debated topic in politics. People from each political party have a wide range of opinions. In 2018, a survey found that seven in ten adults are in favor of stricter gun control laws. Another poll found that 58 percent of people believe gun ownership increases public safety.[10]

An AP/NORC poll found that about six in ten people support a ban on AR-15-style rifles, too. For political parties, 90 percent of Democrats and 50 percent of Republicans are in favor of stricter gun control laws. Americans, however, are less certain that elected leaders will make any laws that limit what guns people can own. About 51 percent of Americans expect politicians to enact tighter gun laws, 42 percent believe there will be no changes, and 6 percent expect fewer strict laws.[11]

because they might eventually join a militia? Should guns be kept in a special location or within people's homes?[12] Because of how laws can be changed and redefined over time, the regulation of guns may be different next year. Questions about various aspects of gun ownership, such as the ability to openly carry a gun, are still under intense debate today.

3

Gun Law in Practice

What do guns laws look like at the different levels of government? There are federal, state, and local laws that help answer the question of who can own a gun. One of the major modern issues is how guns are affecting schools. Were the guns used in a school shooting legally obtained? How does the government regulate hunting tools versus assault weapons?

Rule of Law

The National Rifle Association of America (NRA) is an organization that fights for gun rights. The group has been around since the late 1800s and is a major force in the gun control debate. According to the NRA, there are twenty thousand gun laws already in place. It cites this number to support its argument that the United States does not need more laws but instead more enforcement of the current ones. However, in 2002 the Center on Urban and Metropolitan Policy at the Brookings Institution found that the actual number is closer to about three hundred federal and state gun laws.[1]

Federal

The Giffords Law Center to Prevent Gun Violence lists the federal gun laws in place. There are laws in place that establish the gun purchasing process among many others. This includes a background check of a gun buyer that examines criminal history and mental health reporting.

The federal Gun Control Act of 1968 specifically prohibits the following people from owning a gun: anyone convicted of a crime punishable by imprisonment for more than one year; fugitives; unlawful users of a controlled substance such as drugs; anyone underage (depending on type of gun); the mentally unstable; those illegally in the United States or with renounced US citizenship; the dishonorably discharged from the military; anyone with a restraining order for danger posed toward another person; and anyone convicted of a misdemeanor offense of domestic violence.[2]

State

States have laws that further prevent certain people from owning guns. Each state, as well as Washington, DC, is different, and laws vary from state to state. According to the Giffords Law Center, the states have four major categories of people who regularly have laws placed upon them to limit their gun ownership rights. These are those who are convicted of violent or gun-related misdemeanors, those who are dangerously mentally ill, those who abuse drugs and/or alcohol, and those who are juvenile offenders.[3]

Some states limit one or more of these groups in varying combinations. For example, Alabama has no laws in place restricting juvenile offenders from owning firearms while Florida does. Georgia, Idaho, Louisiana, and others have no state laws prohibiting these groups from owning guns. On the other hand, states including California, Hawaii, Maryland, Massachusetts, and Pennsylvania have laws for each group. Some states, including Indiana and Mississippi, have laws that limit specifically only

President Bill Clinton signs the Brady Bill, with James Brady at his side. Brady was shot alongside President Ronald Regan in 1981. The bill establishes a waiting period and background checks for handgun purchases.

handguns. For example, those who abuse alcohol in Indiana may not purchase and possess a handgun but are free to purchase and possess rifles and shotguns.[4]

Local

Some cities have passed local laws to regulate guns in additional ways. Deerfield, Illinois, has an ordinance in place that bans assault weapons and penalizes citizens who do not forfeit or secure weapons that fall in that category. The Chicago suburb fines a person $200 to $1,000 each day they do not forfeit or secure their weapon.[5]

After the shooting at Marjory Stoneman Douglas High School in Florida, students organized antigun marches and protests, calling for gun reform.

Lincoln, Nebraska, voted to ban bump stocks from the city. A bump stock is a gun accessory that allows people to shoot semiautomatic weapons more quickly. Bump stocks mimic automatic firing, which is considered illegal on the federal level.[6]

In Schools

School shootings are a tragic part of American history. The first campus shooting was reported on November 15, 1840, by the *Richmond Enquirer*. The newspaper reported that University of Virginia law professor John A. G. Davis was shot in front of his dwelling by an unknown person. Schools have been the scene of numerous shootings since, including Columbine High School on April 20, 1999[7], and Marjory Stoneman Douglas High School in Parkland, Florida, on February 14, 2018.

Federal and state laws establish schools as gun-free zones. The Gun-Free School Zones Act of 1990 prohibits any person from knowingly possessing a firearm in a school zone, including 1,000 feet (305 meters) from school grounds. However, the law does not prohibit people from carrying guns in a school if they are licensed by a state or city to possess a gun. If licensed, a person can carry a gun into a school as long as it is unloaded and in a locked container or the gun has been approved by the school.[8] The Gun-Free Schools Act (GFSA), enacted in 1994, focuses on students. Students are automatically expelled from school for at least one year if they bring a gun to or possess one at school.[9]

Guns used for hunting are usually very different from guns used within urban environments; how does the Constitution impact their ownership?

Youth In Revolt

The gun control debate took a new turn following the shooting at Marjory Stoneman Douglas High School. Rather than allowing themselves to be victims, survivors from the school started the #NeverAgain movement to address gun violence in schools.

Led by students including Jaclyn Corin, Alex Wind, Emma Gonzalez, Cameron Kasky, and David Hogg, the grassroots movement focuses on gun reform. They call for changes such as a renewed assault weapons ban, universal background checks, and digitized gun-ownership records.[10] The group organized the March for Our Lives protests in March 2018, which saw over two million participants. Centered in Washington, DC, the march included more than 850 related marches around the world.[11] The group's goal was for four out of five young people to vote in the November 2018 midterm elections. "Either have the politicians pass legislation or set them up to be voted out," said Kasky.[12]

Hunting Weapons

President Barack Obama was careful to respect hunting and the rights of hunters to own firearms. He pointed out that "the reality of guns in urban areas are very different from the realities of guns in rural areas."[13]

Hunters themselves do not all agree on how to proceed with gun laws. Those who have embraced gun controls on semiautomatic weapons have been faced with difficulties. For example, hunting journalist Jim Zumbo lost his magazine job after writing, "I see no place for these weapons among our hunting fraternity," for *Outdoor Life* magazine.[14] The laws have been thus far unsuccessful for both sides of the gun control debate.

4

Ownership

While laws determine who can legally own a gun, there are other laws that specify when, where, and how a person can carry their firearm. Laws also require gun purchasers and sellers to follow several steps before the transaction can be completed.

Buying Guns

The only legal ways to buy a firearm are from a federally licensed gun store, a pawn shop, or another person. Internet sales are handled through licensed firearms dealers. There were more than 54,000 licensed dealers in the United States in 2014, which was a 14 percent increase from 2008. However, there were more than 248,000 licensed firearms dealers in 1992.[1]

There are almost 8,000 licensed pawn shops in the United States, and there are anywhere from 2,000 to 5,200 gun shows held in the United States every year. A gun show allows licensed dealers to sell their products to show attendees.[2] Sellers at gun shows must be federally licensed just as any store would be. However, a loophole exists that allows private collectors to buy, sell, and trade guns without a federal license. Sales of firearms between two people who live in the same state are allowed by law. Private collectors at a gun show fall under this law. This means that background checks are not required when someone buys from a person at a gun show.[3]

Background Checks

A background check helps identify who can and cannot purchase a firearm. The Brady Act, enacted in 1993, saw the creation of the National Instant Criminal Background Check System (NICS) by the FBI. The NICS is a centralized catalog of records about a person's criminal and mental health histories, as well as civil orders, such as a domestic violence restraining order. An individual must not be a convicted felon or fugitive in order to obtain a gun.[4] Each state in the United States has its own set of background check laws. Many allow those with a concealed weapon permit to bypass background checks. Two states, Minnesota and Rhode Island, require

Gun stores across the United States must follow specific laws when it comes to the selling of weapons. Purchasers must undergo background checks and register and license their weapons.

an independent background check where dealers must contact the FBI directly.[5] Background checks have shown to be effective at keeping guns from dangerous or prohibited people. Since 1994, more than 3 million people have been denied a firearm or permit.[6]

A 2017 study estimated that about 22 percent of gun owners' most recent firearms were acquired without a background check. According to another study by the *New England Journal of Medicine*, the leading source of guns used in crimes is the private-party gun market.[7] Several states introduced their own laws requiring background checks in sales between private individuals, such as at a gun show. These states include California, New York, Pennsylvania, and Washington. Illinois specifically requires background checks before the sale or transfer of a firearm at a gun show.[8]

Registration

People must register their firearms. This means a person must have a designated law enforcement agency record their ownership of a firearm. Doing so allows law enforcement to "identify, disarm, and prosecute violent criminals and people illegally in possession of firearms." It also helps law enforcement know if there might be firearms present at a location.[9] Registration differs from state to state and may include a person's name, address, and other identifying information. Information about the gun that must be recorded includes manufacturer, importer, model, and serial number.[10]

If a gun is involved in a crime, police officers can trace where the gun came from and who its previous owners were. If a firearm is lost or stolen, law enforcement must be alerted to help keep their records current. Gun owners must renew their registration every year. If a person becomes

prohibited from owning a gun, if for example they are convicted of a crime, then law enforcement will have to ability to remove their weapons.[11]

Registration laws are in place to help discourage illegal gun sales. If a gun owner sells or trades their firearm to a dangerous individual, law enforcement will be able to trace the weapon back to them. Registration

Licensing

Getting a gun license means being legally allowed to own, purchase, or sell a firearm. Some licenses also require gun owners to pass safety tests. Federal law does not require gun owners or purchasers to be licensed. Licensing laws differ from state to state, and many states have no licensing laws in any form.[12]

States including Connecticut and New Jersey require a license for all types of guns, while others such as New York and North Carolina require licensing only for handguns. Similarly, safety training or an exam are required in only a handful of states, including Massachusetts and Rhode Island.[13]

also discourages people buying guns for people who are not eligible for gun ownership since the buyer will have to register as the owner.

However, there is no national system of gun registration. Two states, Hawaii and the District of Columbia, require all firearms be registered, while New York requires handguns to be registered. Other states, including Delaware, Florida, and South Dakota, prohibit firearm registries. This means no firearms are registered in these states since there are also no federal laws requiring registration. New California or Maryland residents are required to report their firearms.[14]

Age Restrictions

Depending on the type of gun, a person may have to be over a certain age to own one. Federal law distinguishes between handguns and long guns

In many cases, federal law may differ from local law when it comes to gun ownership; age and the kind of weapon are both possible factors.

such as rifles and shotguns. Handguns and handgun ammunition may not be possessed by anyone under eighteen. There is no minimum age requirement for long guns or long gun ammunition.[15]

State laws can be categorized by purchase and possession of a handgun or a long gun. Some states, such as Alabama, have a minimum age of eighteen for the purchase and possession of a handgun while having no age restrictions for long guns. Other states require parental consent to possess a long gun. The youngest minimum age is in Minnesota, which allows fourteen-year-olds to possess a long gun with a firearms safety certificate. Some states, including Kansas, Kentucky, and Mississippi, have no minimum age requirement for any type of firearm purchase or possession.[16]

5

In Politics

Gun ownership is a major topic in US politics. With recent shootings in schools and public places, many are calling for stricter gun laws. However, many do not see the need for more gun laws, believing that the Second Amendment is under attack.

School Zones

The United States, without question, has had more school shootings than any other major industrialized nation. An industrialized country is one with a developed economy, infrastructure such as roads and highways, and a high standard of living. Of all such countries, the United States has had fifty-seven times more school shootings than any other country. Since 2009, the United States has had 288 school shootings compared to two each for Canada and France. The next closest country is Mexico with eight.[1]

With such shocking numbers, it is no surprise that reducing this number is a major goal for some politicians. Laws are already in place to discourage people and students from bringing guns to school. For example, the District of Columbia and all but one state, Massachusetts, immediately expel students from school for at least one year.[2] Many feel that the Gun-Free School Zones Act of 1990 is just the first step toward better gun laws.

Political Divide

Following the school shooting at Marjory Stoneman Douglas High School in Parkland, Florida, gun control became a major topic in US politics. Some elected officials suggested more laws to ban assault weapons, while others avoided the topic altogether. Florida Senate president Joe Negron said, "My focus is on making sure that lawful citizens who are obeying the law and entitled to their constitutional rights have appropriate access to firearms."[3]

The US gun control debate is generally between the two major political parties, the Republicans and the Democrats. Highlighting the divide,

The United States has more school shootings than any nation in the world. More and more, students are protesting to say they have had enough of such violence in their halls.

Republican president Donald Trump ended a law by former Democratic president Barack Obama that kept some categories of mentally ill citizens from buying guns.[4] In the past, Democratic candidates avoided the gun control issue in states dominated by the Republican Party. Their strategy was to not alienate voters who would typically disagree with their views on firearms. However, the high number of school shootings has some Democrats changing their strategy. Robert Spitzer, political scientist at the State University of New York at Cortland said, "Political rallying of the Parkland students and their allies have gotten more Democrats to embrace a gun safety agenda."[5]

The Republican Party strongly supports the Second Amendment and the right of US citizens to own firearms. With strong backing from the National Rifle Association, it would like to reduce the number of gun control laws. However, the party states that reducing gun violence also falls within its agenda. Following the Parkland shooting, Republican senator John Cornyn of Texas worked with Democrats to strengthen background-check rules.[6]

Government Protection

The Bureau of Alcohol, Tobacco, Firearms and Explosives (ATF) is a law enforcement agency. As part of the United States' Department of Justice, the ATF is responsible for protecting citizens from illegal use of firearms as well as explosives, bombings, terrorism, and more.

The ATF investigates people it deems dangerous, including armed violent offenders and career criminals, drug traffickers, violent gangs, and firearms dealers. By targeting these groups, the ATF aims to reduce violent crime. The ATF issues firearms licenses, conducts firearms licensee qualification and compliance inspections, and aids the enforcement of gun purchasing laws.[7] The ATF also assists law enforcement in identifying and apprehending those who have illegally purchased a gun. With the ATF's

Emma Gonzales (*center*), a student at Marjory Stoneman Douglas High School in Florida, led the March for Our Lives in Washington, DC, in March 2018.

inspections, tracing guns becomes more successful due to the training it provides licensees in proper record keeping and business practices.[8]

At Home

Domestic violence, or violence that takes place in one's home, becomes deadly when guns are involved. According to the Giffords Law Center, domestic violence assaults are twelve times more likely to result in death once a gun becomes involved. The violence is particularly dangerous for women. Further statistics show that women in the United States are sixteen times more likely to be murdered by a gun than in other developed countries. In 2011, almost two-thirds of women killed with guns were killed by their spouse or partner.[9]

The federal government has some laws in place to address domestic gun violence. For example, anyone convicted of a "misdemeanor crime of domestic violence" or subject to certain domestic violence protective orders is not allowed to purchase and possess firearms and ammunition under the Lautenberg Amendment of 1996. A misdemeanor crime is defined as the use or attempted use of physical force or threatened use of a deadly weapon as an element. From November 30, 1998, to July 31, 2014, the FBI found that more than 109,000 people were denied a firearm purchase because of the Lautenberg Amendment.[10]

The Bureau of Alcohol, Tobacco, Firearms, and Explosives is responsible for protecting citizens from illegal use of firearms as well as explosives, bombings, and terrorism.

Mental Health and Guns

Many politicians, including President Trump and Florida governor Rick Scott believe that mental health is a reason for the rise of gun violence in the United States, particularly in schools. The Parkland, Florida, shooting led the government under President Trump to blame poor mental health services. Alex Azar, the Health and Human Services secretary, said the department would be focused on the mental health issue moving forward.[11]

Many doctors disagree with the idea that mental health is the reason behind the increase in violence. Dr. Louis Kraus, forensic psychiatry chief at Chicago's Rush University Medical College, told the Associated Press, "The concept that mental illness is a precursor to violent behavior is nonsense. The vast majority of gun violence is not attributable to mental illness."[12]

In some states, law enforcement is required to remove at least some firearms at the scene of a domestic violence incident where guns are present. These states include Montana, Oklahoma, and West Virginia. Federal laws do not address domestic abusers who are with a partner but are not married, live together, or share a child. This is known as the "boyfriend loophole." Twenty-three states address this gap in the law, including Delaware, Louisiana, and Texas.[13]

While the government decides on the best path forward, the threat of gun violence at home or at a public space will have to be addressed as the country moves to the future.

6

The World of Tomorrow

As gun ownership continues, the future may hold drastic changes for laws and regulations. Laws in other countries could provide a blueprint for the United States when it comes to regulating gun ownership in a way that most people agree is reasonable. Technology introduces a new challenge to lawmakers looking to keep guns away from criminals and those with mental health issues.

International Law

In Mexico, the United States' southern neighbor, citizens are allowed to own handguns and hunting rifles for self-defense and sport. However, there is only one place in the entire country where Mexicans can purchase a gun. A provision or requirement in the law gives the government the power to choose the types of weapons allowed and under what conditions. Mexicans can buy one handgun for home protection, while hunting and shooting club members can own up to nine rifles under a certain size depending on the firearm. The lone gun store in Mexico is located on an army base in the capital and is heavily guarded.[1] Despite these measures, there have been more than 164,000 killings from 2007 to 2014 in Mexico.

The entire country of Mexico has only one authorized gun shop for anyone who wants to buy a gun. The government controls what kinds of weapons can be sold.

Most of these firearms were purchased illegally from black market dealers bringing in guns from America.[2]

In Canada, buying a gun requires a twenty-eight-day waiting period and a background check more detailed than the ones conducted in the United States. Gun owners must also take a safety training course. Canada classifies firearms into three groups. Non-restricted weapons include ordinary rifles and shotguns. Restricted weapons include handguns, as well as semiautomatic rifles and shotguns. Prohibited weapons include automatic weapons. There is a ban on large-capacity containers that hold ammunition, known as magazines. Military-style guns and ammunition are also banned. Since 2012, Canadians do not have to register handguns with the government.[3]

Japan has one of the lowest gun homicide rates in the world at one in ten million people. The country has made most guns illegal, and ownership rates are low. The only guns people are allowed to own include shotguns, air guns, guns used in competition, and guns used for research or industrial purposes. Even owning one of these allowable weapons requires formal instruction and passing written, mental, and drug tests in addition to a thorough background check. Authorities must also be informed of how gun owners intend to store their guns and ammunition. Gun owners must have their firearms inspected every year.[4]

3D Printers

3D printing is a way for people to turn digital files containing three-dimensional data into physical objects. There are various ways 3D printing works. Some printers spray a liquid that hardens into a specific shape, while others use a laser to trace an object layer by layer. Originally invented in the mid-1980s by Charles W. Hull, 3D printing has evolved from an expensive technology into one that people can own at home.[5]

How 2018 Could Change the Laws

Following school shootings in Parkland, Florida, and Santa Fe High School in Santa Fe, Texas, the 2018 midterm elections in the United States saw a dramatic shift when it comes to gun control and support of it.[6] Democratic candidates, historically for gun control, focused on reducing gun violence in America. Although the way they present their side has changed from "gun controls" to "common-sense reforms," the ultimate goal of more gun restrictions remains the same.[7]

Republicans, historically for gun rights, have expressed doubt over the Democratic campaign strategy. Joseph Ax and Time Reid of Reuters reported US representative Steve Chabot of Ohio saying, "I don't think anyone knows if it's going to have an impact" on the election. Chabot is unconvinced more gun restrictions will prevent violence.[8]

Technology now allows for the 3D printing of guns. That is exactly what gun-printing advocacy group Defense Distributed intends to bring to US citizens. Originally, the federal courts prohibited the group from posting iys designs for a 3D printed gun online where anyone could download and print their own working gun. However, the law does not prevent it from selling gun *blueprints* to US citizens. Due to US export law, it cannot sell its designs to non-US citizens.[9]

Twenty states have sued the federal government to prevent Defense Distributed, or anyone else, from sharing 3D firearm blueprints online. They believe that the guns could easily end up in the hands of dangerous people who would normally be prohibited from owning a traditional gun.

3D printers have changed the gun landscape yet again; what becomes of the laws when people can print their own weapons in their own homes?

As of 2018, the issue is far from being resolved. Gun-rights supporters will still fight legal challenges and hope to share the blueprints with anyone they wish. Meanwhile, gun-control advocates will not be happy until 3D-printed guns are no longer available online.[10]

Tomorrow and Beyond

Antonio Garcia Martinez of *Wired* notes that the very definition of guns is changing. Gun owners, Martinez says, are free to modify their weapons or even build their own at home. Since the pieces to build a weapon are considered "accessories," owners are not required to report anything.[11]

Fifty-nine people died at the 2017 Route 91 Harvest Music Festival mass shooting in Las Vegas. The shooter used an accessory known as a bump stock that effectively made his weapon automatic. While the federal government has been slow to act on a bump stock ban despite President Trump's insistence, bump stocks have been banned in several states.[12]

The question of who can own a gun has a complicated answer. The United States' Founding Fathers are no longer around to shed light on exactly what they meant in the Second Amendment. An eye-opening number of public shootings have made the topic even more relevant since anyone is seemingly at risk. New technology complicates the issue in modern America. There could easily be more issues as science and technology advance and the nation's laws adapt to keep up with the times.

Chapter Notes

Introduction

1. Christopher Ingraham, "Analysis | There Are More Guns than People in the United States, According to a New Study of Global Firearm Ownership," *Washington Post*, June 19, 2018, https://www.washingtonpost.com/news/wonk/wp/2018/06/19/there-are-more-guns-than-people-in-the-united-states-according-to-a-new-study-of-global-firearm-ownership/?noredirect=on&utm_term=.39cc2f915535.
2. Ibid.
3. Ibid.
4. Ibid.

Chapter 1. The Constitution

1. "The Constitution," the White House, https://www.whitehouse.gov/about-the-white-house/the-constitution.
2. Ibid.
3. Ibid.
4. Ibid.
5. Jill K. Mulhall, *Causes of the Revolution* (Huntington Beach, CA: Teacher Created Materials, 2005).
6. Ibid.
7. Ibid.
8. Ryan Strasser, "Second Amendment," LII / Legal Information Institute, June 05, 2017, https://www.law.cornell.edu/wex/second_amendment.
9. Ibid.
10. Ibid.

Chapter 2. The Gun Amendment

1. Luis Acosta, "United States: Gun Ownership and the Supreme Court," June 26, 2005, http://www.loc.gov/law/help/second-amendment.php.
2. Ibid.
3. Ibid.
4. Meagan Flynn and Fred Barbash, "Analysis | Does the Second Amendment Really Protect Assault Weapons? Four Courts Have Said No," *Washington Post*, February 22, 2018, https://www.washingtonpost.com/news/morning-mix/wp/2018/02/22/

does-the-second-amendment-really-protect-assault-weapons-four-courts-have-said-no/?utm_term=.9dda62ee0170.

5. Jeff Daniels, "Definition of What's Actually an 'Assault Weapon' Is a Highly Contentious Issue," CNBC, February 27, 2018, https://www.cnbc.com/2018/02/21/definition-of-whats-an-assault-weapon-is-a-very-contentious-issue.html.

6. Ibid.

7. Ibid.

8. AJ Willingham, "Deconstructing the Second Amendment," CNN, March 28, 2018, https://www.cnn.com/2016/08/10/politics/what-does-the-second-amendment-actually-mean-trnd/index.html.

9. Ibid.

10. Emily Swanson, "Americans' Views on Guns, Gun Control Is Evolving: Polls," NBC Chicago, March 23, 2018, https://www.nbcchicago.com/news/national-international/Gun-Control-Law-Support-Rising-Polls-477730753.html.

11. Ibid.

12. Glen Martin, "So, About That 'Well-Regulated Militia' Part of the Constitution," Cal Alumni Association, August 29, 2017, https://alumni.berkeley.edu/california-magazine/just-in/2017-08-28/so-about-well-regulated-militia-part-constitution.

Chapter 3. Gun Law in Practice

1. Lauren Fox, "Four Gun Claims That Are Just Plain Wrong," *U.S. News & World* Report, February 1, 2013, https://www.usnews.com/news/articles/2013/02/01/four-gun-claims-that-are-just-plain-wrong.

2. "Categories of Prohibited People," Giffords Law Center to Prevent Gun Violence, http://lawcenter.giffords.org/gun-laws/policy-areas/who-can-have-a-gun/categories-of-prohibited-people/#federal.

3. Ibid.

4. Ibid.

5. Madison Park, "New Jersey Is One of the Latest States to Enact New Gun Control Measures," CNN, June 13, 2018, https://www.cnn.com/2018/04/09/us/gun-laws-since-parkland/index.html.

6. Ibid.

7. Michael S. Rosenwald, *Washington Post*, "159 Years Before Columbine, the Nation's First School Shooting Happened at UVa," WJLA, April 29, 2018, https://wjla.com/news/local/159-years-columbine-nations-first-school-shooting-happened-uva.

8. "Guns in Schools," Giffords Law Center to Prevent Gun Violence, http://lawcenter.giffords.org/gun-laws/policy-areas/guns-in-public/guns-in-schools/.

9. Ibid.

10. Charlotte Alter, "How Parkland Teens Are Leading the Gun Control Conversation," *Time*, March 22, 2018, http://time.com/longform/never-again-movement/.

11. Ryan Sit, "More than 2 Million Joined March for Our Lives Protests in 90 Percent of US Voting Districts," *Newsweek*, March 26, 2018, https://www.newsweek.com/march-our-lives-how-many-2-million-90-voting-district-860841.

12. Alter, *Time*.

13. Matt Williams, "Obama: Gun Control Advocates Must Respect Rural Hunting Culture," *The Guardian*, January 27, 2013, https://www.theguardian.com/world/2013/jan/27/obama-gun-control-hunting-culture.

14. Jamie Tarabay, "Hunters: Gun Rights Have Nothing to Do with Hunting," Al Jazeera America, June 18, 2014, http://america.aljazeera.com/articles/2014/6/18/hunters-gun-right-shavenothingtodowithhunting.html.

Chapter 4. Ownership

1. Gregory Korte, "Buying a Gun Legally in the US Isn't Difficult," *USA Today*, June 21, 2015, https://www.usatoday.com/story/news/nation/2015/06/20/how-to-legally-buy-a-gun-in-the-united-states/29034879/.

2. Ibid.

3. Ibid.

4. "Background Check Procedures," Giffords Law Center to Prevent Gun Violence, http://lawcenter.giffords.org/gun-laws/policy-areas/background-checks/background-check-procedures/.

5. Ibid.

6. "Universal Background Checks," Giffords Law Center to Prevent Gun Violence, http://lawcenter.giffords.org/gun-laws/policy-areas/background-checks/universal-background-checks/.

7. Ibid.

8. Ibid.

9. "Registration," Giffords Law Center to Prevent Gun Violence, http://lawcenter.giffords.org/gun-laws/policy-areas/gun-owner-responsibilities/registration/.

10. Ibid.

11. Ibid.

12. "Licensing," Giffords Law Center to Prevent Gun Violence, http://lawcenter.giffords.org/gun-laws/policy-areas/gun-owner-responsibilities/licensing/.Ibid.

13. Ibid.

14. Ibid.

15. "Minimum Age to Purchase & Possess," Giffords Law Center to Prevent Gun Violence, http://lawcenter.giffords.org/gun-laws/policy-areas/who-can-have-a-gun/minimum-age/.

16. Ibid.

Chapter 5. In Politics

1. Chip Grabow and Lisa Rose, "The US Has Had 57 Times as Many School Shootings as the Other Major Industrialized Nations Combined," CNN, May 21, 2018, https://www.cnn.com/2018/05/21/us/school-shooting-us-versus-world-trnd/index.html.

2. "Guns in Schools," Giffords Law Center to Prevent Gun Violence, http://lawcenter.giffords.org/gun-laws/policy-areas/guns-in-public/guns-in-schools/.

3. *Miami Herald* Editorial Board, "These Politicians Have Dodged the Issue of Gun Control. We Call BS — and You Should, Too," *Miami Herald*, February 20, 2018, https://www.miamiherald.com/opinion/editorials/article201113684.html.

4. Ibid.

5. Emma Newburger, "Former Gun-friendly Democrats Will Put Their Newfound NRA Opposition to the Test This Fall," CNBC, September 19, 2018, https://www.cnbc.com/2018/09/18/former-pro-gun-democrats-reject-the-nra-and-triumph-in-primaries.html.

6. Philip Elliott and W. J. Hennigan, "Inside Republicans' New Direction on Gun Restrictions," *Time*, March 1, 2018, http://time.com/5180537/gun-control-donald-trump-meeting/.

7. "Firearms," Bureau of Alcohol, Tobacco, Firearms and Explosives, https://www.atf.gov/firearms.

8. Ibid.

9. "Domestic Violence & Firearms," Giffords Law Center to Prevent Gun Violence, http://lawcenter.giffords.org/gun-laws/policy-areas/who-can-have-a-gun/domestic-violence-firearms/.

10. Ibid.

11. Associated Press, "Trump Said Mental Illness Leads to Gun Violence. Here's Why Doctors Disagree," PBS, February 19, 2018, https://www.pbs.org/newshour/health/trump-said-mental-illness-leads-to-gun-violence-heres-why-doctors-disagree.

12. Ibid.

13. Ibid.

Chapter 6. The World of Tomorrow

1. The Associated Press, "Mexicans Have the Right to Own Guns, but Few Do," CBS News, August 17, 2016, https://www.cbsnews.com/news/mexicans-have-the-right-to-own-guns-but-few-do/.

2. Ibid.

3. Jonathan Masters, "How Do US Gun Laws Compare to Other Countries?" PBS, June 13, 2016, https://www.pbs.org/newshour/nation/how-do-u-s-gun-laws-compare-to-other-countries.

4. Ibid.

5. Tony Hoffman, "3D Printing: What You Need to Know," PCMAG, June 20, 2018, https://www.pcmag.com/article2/0,2817,2394720,00.asp.

6. German Lopez, "The 2018 Midterm Elections May Have Exposed a Shift on Gun Control," November 7, 2018, https://www.vox.com/2018/11/7/18072146/midterm-election-gun-control-ballot-initiative-congress-results.

7. Joseph Ax, "Democratic Candidates Embrace Gun Control Despite Political Risks," Reuters, July 30, 2018, https://www.reuters.com/article/us-usa-election-guncontrol-insight/democratic-candidates-embrace-gun-control-despite-political-risks-idUSKBN1KK134.

8. Ibid.

9. Emily Dreyfuss, "3-D Printed Gun Blueprints Are Back, and Only New Laws Can Stop Them," *Wired*, September 04, 2018, https://www.wired.com/story/3-d-printed-gun-blueprints-return-laws-injunction/.

10. Ibid.

11. Antonio García Martínez, "How 3-D Printing Exposes the Fallacy of Federal Gun Laws," *Wired*, August 15, 2018, https://www.wired.com/story/defense-distributed-3d-printing-exposes-fallacy-of-federal-gun-laws/.

12. "Opinion: A Year after the Las Vegas Shooting, Congress Still Hasn't Banned Bump Stocks," *Washington Post*, October 02, 2018, https://www.washingtonpost.com/opinions/a-year-after-the-las-vegas-shooting-congress-still-hasnt-banned-bump-stocks/2018/10/02/88e72380-c5b9-11e8-b2b5-79270f9cce17_story.html?utm_term=.3db6ced02d33.

Glossary

assault weapon An automatic or semiautomatic firearm.

background check The process of looking up a person's criminal and mental health records.

civilian A person not belonging to the armed services or police.

domestic violence Violent or aggressive behavior that takes place at home and usually involves a spouse or partner.

due process Fair treatment through the judicial system.

federal Relating to the central government of the United States.

firearm A portable gun such as a rifle or pistol.

intention An aim or plan.

magazine A container in a gun for holding cartridges.

militia An organized force of nonmilitary citizens meant to supplement a regular army in an emergency.

ordinance A piece of legislation or law enacted by a city or town authority.

prohibit To formally forbid something by law.

provision A condition or requirement in a legal document.

register To enter or record on an official list or directory.

Further Reading

Books

Merino, Noel. *Gun Violence.* Farmington Hills, MI: Greenhaven Press, a Part of Gale, Cengage Learning, 2015.

Nakaya, Andrea C. *Thinking Critically: Mass Shootings.* San Diego, CA: ReferencePoint Press, 2015.

Wolny, Philip. *Gun Rights: Interpreting the Constitution.* New York, NY: Rosen Publishing Group, 2015.

Websites

Ben's Guide to the US Government

bensguide.gpo.gov/j-us-constitution

Ben's Guide educates children and educators about the government, the Constitution, the Bill of Rights, and more.

Project ChildSafe

projectchildsafe.org

Project ChildSafe is a US-based firearm safety education program developed by the National Shooting Sports Foundation.

Index